Written by Noah Leatherland

BASEBALL

PowerKiDS press

Published in 2025
by The Rosen Publishing Group, Inc.
2544 Clinton Street, Buffalo, NY 14224

© 2024 BookLife Publishing Ltd.

Written by: Noah Leatherland
Edited by: E.C. Andrews
Designed by: Jasmine Pointer

Cataloging-in-Publication Data

Names: Leatherland, Noah, 1999-.
Title: Baseball / Noah Leatherland.
Description: Buffalo, NY : PowerKids Press, 2025. | Series: World of sports | Includes glossary and index.
Identifiers: ISBN 9781499448924 (pbk.) | ISBN 9781499448931 (library bound) | ISBN 9781499448948 (ebook)
Subjects: LCSH: Baseball--Juvenile literature.
Classification: LCC GV867.5 L384 2025 | DDC 796.357--dc23

Manufactured in the United States of America

CPSIA Compliance Information: Batch #CW25PK. For further information contact Rosen Publishing at 1-800-237-9932.

Find us on

IMAGE CREDITS

CONTENTS

WORDS THAT LOOK LIKE THIS CAN BE FOUND IN THE GLOSSARY ON PAGE 24.

PLAY BALL!

Everyone can take part in sports. Playing sports helps you learn how to work as part of a team. It can also help you grow stronger and faster. Do you have a favorite sport?

Baseball is said to be the United States' favorite <u>pastime</u>. Baseball takes a lot of teamwork. In order to win, players need to be able to <u>communicate</u> with each other.

THE BASICS

A game of baseball is played by two teams of nine players. A game is made up of nine innings. In an inning, both teams have a turn at batting.

Baseball teams have **substitute** players that can swap in.

When a player hits the ball, they can run to the bases. A point is scored when a player manages to run through all the bases and return to home base.

POSITIONS

Batting

Every player has a turn at batting. Their job is to hit the ball that is thrown at them by the <u>opponent</u>. Once they hit the ball, they run for the bases.

Players have different positions when their team is pitching and fielding. They can be placed on one of the bases, in the infield, or in the outfield.

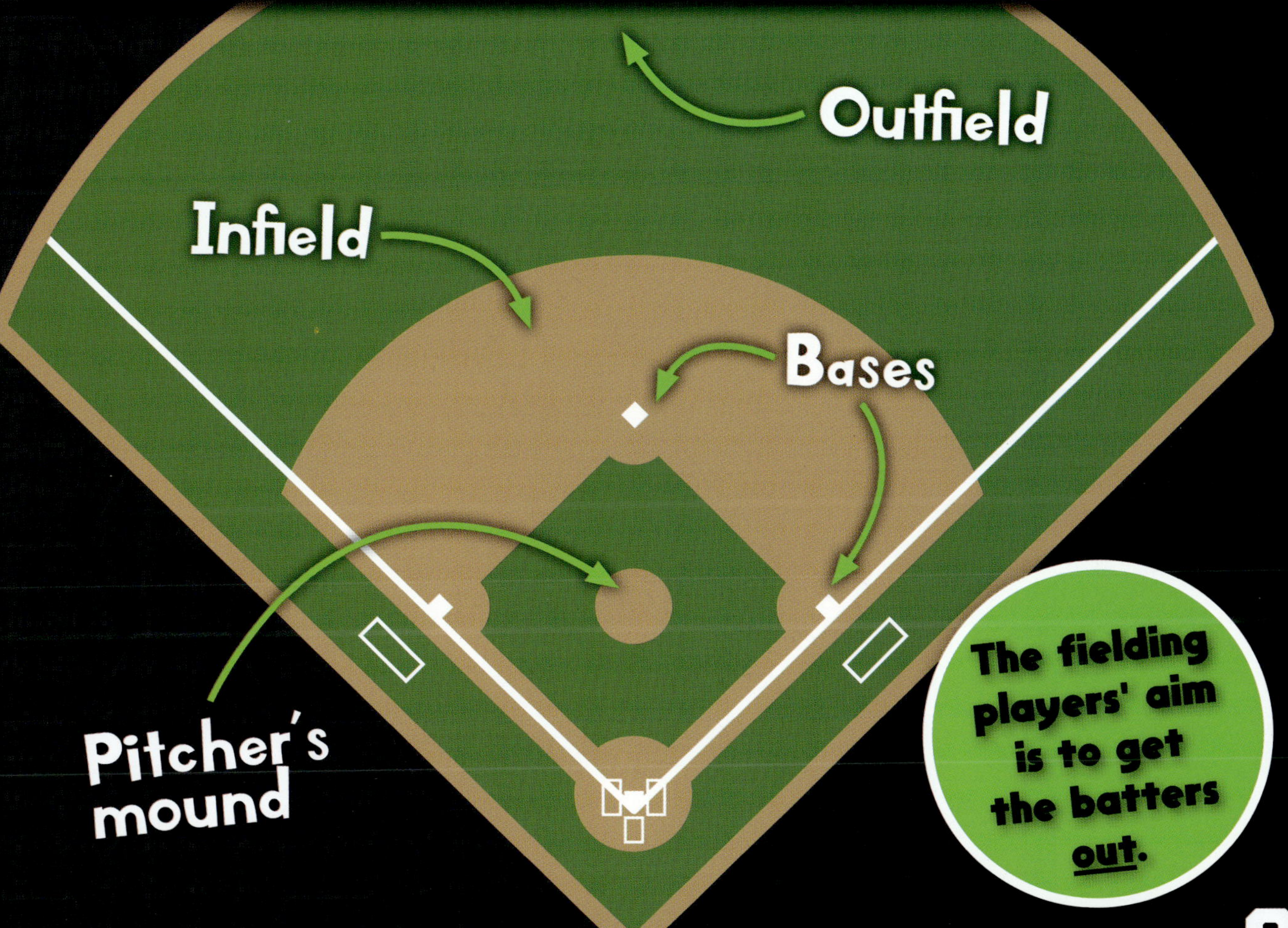

Pitcher

The pitcher stands on the pitcher's mound. They throw the ball towards the batter. Pitchers try to get batters out with three strikes. A strike happens when the batter misses the ball.

Catcher

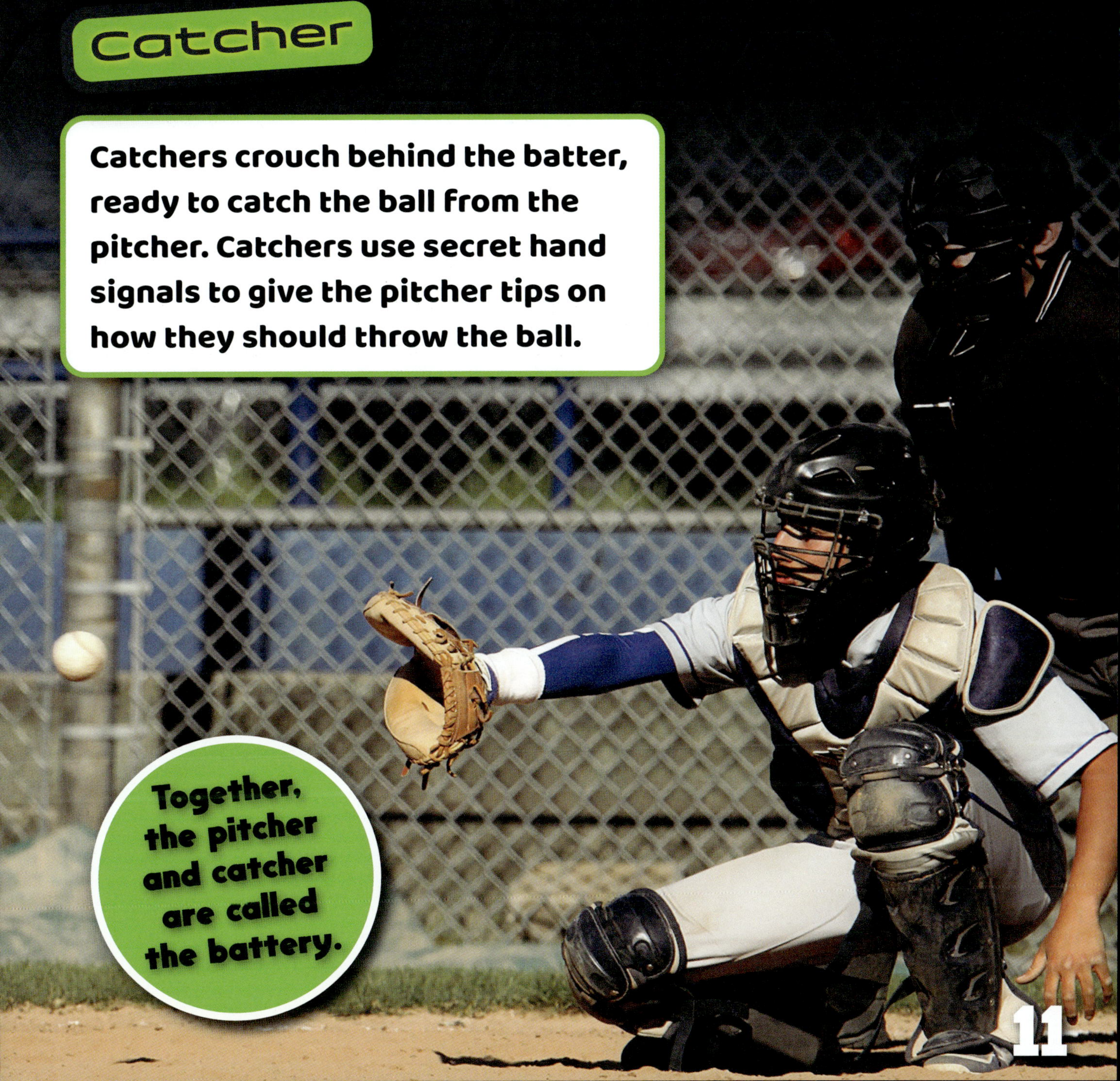

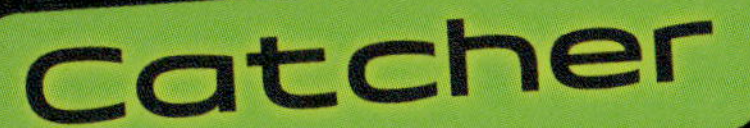

Catchers crouch behind the batter, ready to catch the ball from the pitcher. Catchers use secret hand signals to give the pitcher tips on how they should throw the ball.

Together, the pitcher and catcher are called the battery.

Infield

Throwing the ball to one of the bases before the opponent can run to them forces the runner out. The fielding team puts players close to each base to help force the runners out.

The infield players the base players and the shortstop.

Outfield

Fielding teams need to be ready in case the batter hits the ball very far. Outfield players catch the balls that have been hit far and throw them to the infielders.

Outfielders get a batter out by catching the ball the batter hit before it lands.

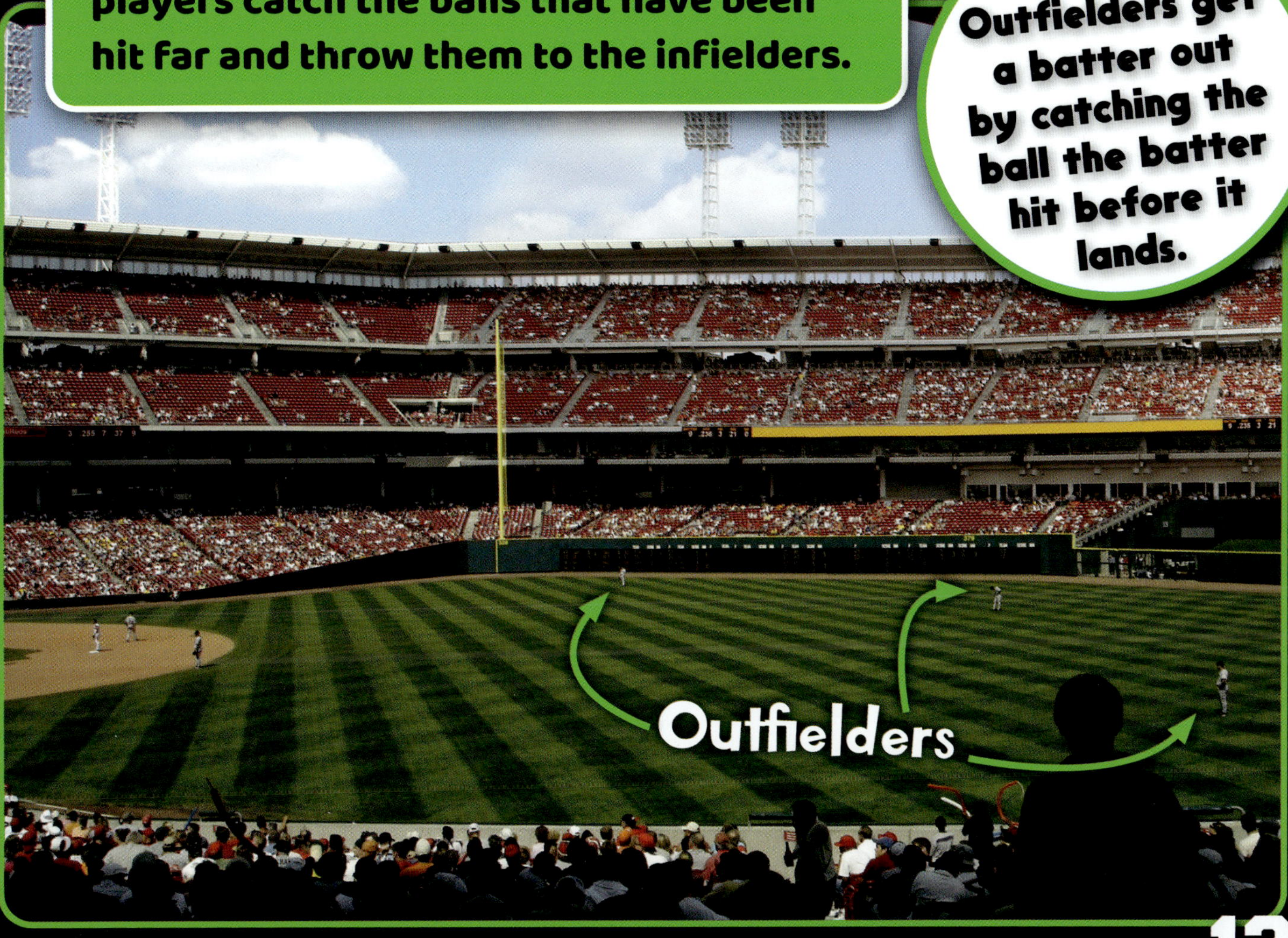

TACTICS

Baseball teams use different <u>tactics</u> to help them score runs and get opponents out. Batters can try to hit the ball towards different parts of the field to help their teammates on the bases.

Pitchers throw the ball in different ways. This can trick the batter and make it hard to hit the ball. Fastballs and curveballs are common pitches. Fastballs move very fast. Curveballs curve in the air.

FOULS

Batters need to hit the ball between the two straight edges of the field. These are called the foul lines. If they hit the ball outside of these lines, it is called a foul ball.

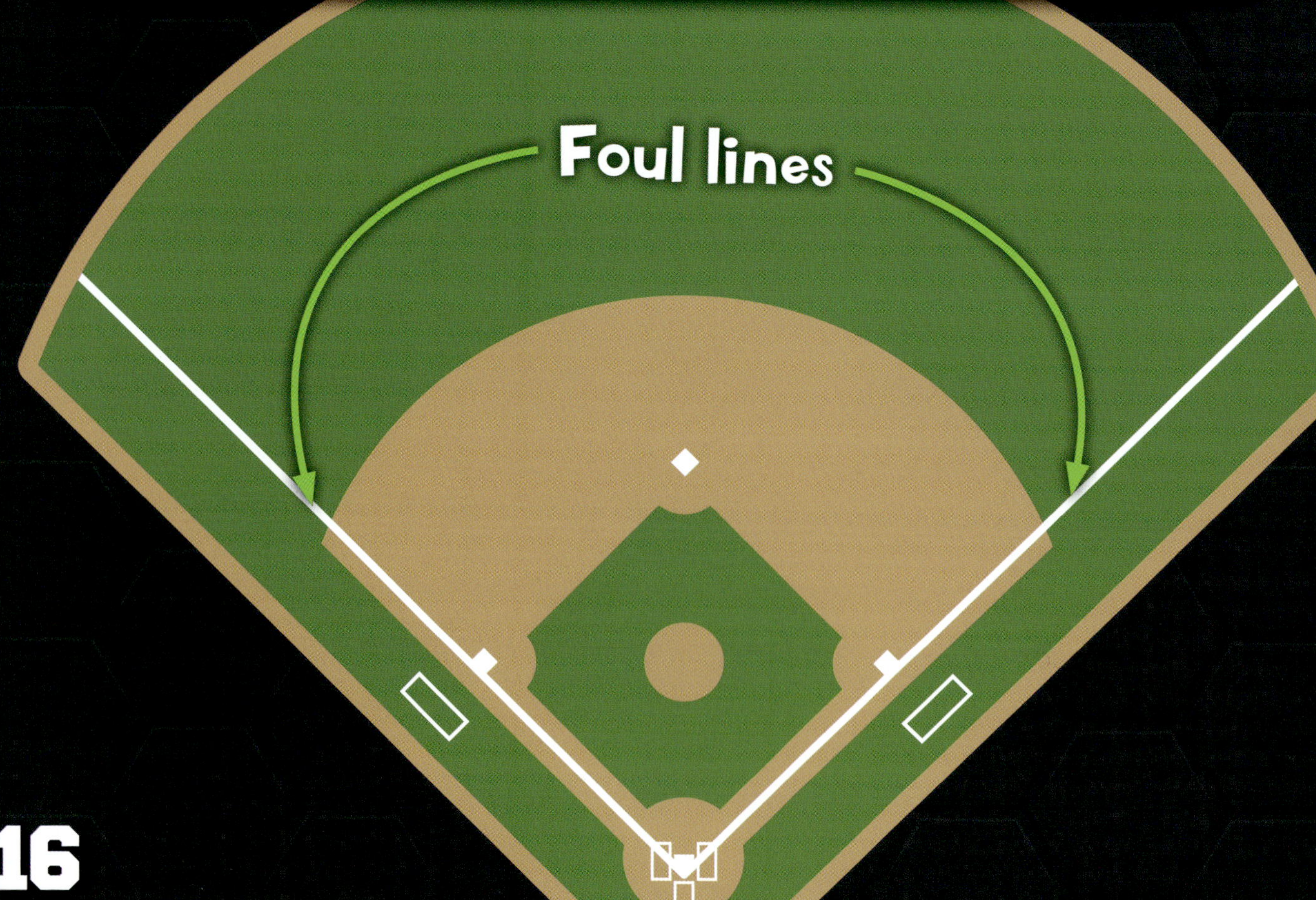
Foul lines

Batters cannot run after they hit a foul ball. Hitting a foul ball can count as a first or a second strike. However, a batter cannot get a third strike for hitting a foul ball.

If a fielder catches a foul ball, the batter is out.

HOME RUNS

If a batter hits the ball really well, they could get a home run. A home run is when a batter hits the ball and runs through all the bases in one try.

Home runs can get a team lots of points. If they have runners on all the bases and someone hits a home run, all the players can run home and earn four points altogether!

THE WORLD SERIES

The World **Series** is the biggest event in baseball. The two top teams in the **MLB** play against each other to decide the champions. Millions of people tune in to watch the World Series.

The two teams play each other in a series of seven games. Whoever wins the most games are the champions! The winners of the World Series are given a big trophy as a prize.

The World Series trophy

WORLD OF SPORTS

You could gather some friends to play a simple game of catch at the park. If you want to play a full game, there are likely some teams near you that need more players!

23

GLOSSARY

common	regularly occurring or often found
communicate	to pass information between two or more things
MLB	Major League Baseball
opponent	the team one is playing against. Also, one player on the team one is playing against.
out	when a player can no longer score points and must leave the field
pastime	something someone does for fun
series	a set number of games played between two teams
substitute	something that replaces something else
tactics	planned ways of doing something

INDEX